# FOUR MURDERED BROTHERS

The true story of one New Orleans family torn apart
by gun violence

By
## ERICA PARKER

*Four Murdered Brothers*
Copyright © 2016 Erica Parker

Book design by:
Arbor Services, Inc.
http://www.arborservices.co/

Printed in the United States

1.Title  2. Author  3. Memoir

ISBN: 978-0-692-77425-0
LCCN: 2016914875

# *Dedication*

This work is dedicated to my four brothers who were taken too
young and too fast. You all are sorely missed.

# Table of Contents

# Chapter One

## *Broken Legacy*

The day my life changed forever began with a road trip—an arduous cross-country move from Tacoma, Washington, to New Orleans, Louisiana.

The summer of 1992 was so hot that the soaring July temperatures and a rash of California earthquakes sent my husband, three of our four kids, and me on the longer eastward route through Colorado rather than cutting southeast into California. My husband, Malcolm, and I made a ragtag two-car convoy—my Pontiac 6000 and Malcolm's blue Oldsmobile, with all of our belongings crammed into a trailer hitched to the back of the Oldsmobile. We communicated to each other by walkie-talkies while driving. The experience was particularly harrowing for me, because I was an inexperienced driver. I had logged only about a year behind the wheel before undertaking the long trip back to Louisiana.

Malcolm and I had originally come to Tacoma in search of a better life for our children. And we found it. Washington had better schools than New Orleans, more job opportunities, and safer communities away from the crime-infested housing projects I had grown up in. My children learned "proper" articulation, speaking more deliberately rather than using the heavily accented English that was typical of Louisiana. Their stronger education would, I hoped, offer them a real shot at a better future.

But we were a long way from our friends and relatives. Several of my female cousins, who reside in Houston, insisted that we should live closer to home. Malcolm and I talked it over and decided that Houston was a good idea.

The plan was to visit our family in New Orleans first, then backtrack to Houston. As a native of New Orleans and the oldest of six children, I was looking forward to seeing my family again for the first time in nearly a year—especially my four brothers: Kimbro (nicknamed "Brody"), Leonard Jr., Leniel, and Lamont. My youngest daughter went ahead of us, and she was staying with my sister Yvonne and my mother in New Orleans as the family awaited our arrival.

What should have been a three-day journey to New Orleans became a weeklong ordeal. The longer route sapped gas and dried up our money. My husband's blue Oldsmobile finally gave out and broke down for the last time. The vehicle was beyond hope, and we had no money to fix it. We hitched the trailer to my Pontiac 6000 and left the decrepit Oldsmobile by the side of the road, abandoned on the highway. Now, with my husband and our three children all in one car, we drove deeper into the South.

When we finally limped into Louisiana in the late evening hours, we were exhausted. The children were restless, drenched in sweat from the oppressive mid-July heat, and stir-crazy from too many hours in the car. It was long past their bedtime. As we drove through the darkness to my mother's house at one a.m., the headlights landed on my sister Yvonne, who was anxiously waving at us and balancing my little niece on her hip.

A mixture of emotions swept over me—relief to be home, gratitude that our difficult trip was over, and a great happiness to see my sister again. I got out of the car and reached for her baby, but Yvonne put her hand on my arm and stopped me.

"Wait, Erica. I need to tell you something . . ."

Still looking at my beautiful little niece, I barely registered that my sister's face was entirely blank. But nothing could have prepared me for what she said next.

"Erica, Brody's just been killed."

I froze. Brody—Kimbro. My oldest brother, Kimbro, had been killed.

The world spun. A hot vortex of humid air rushed around me and everything went black. I passed out on the pavement.

When I came to, I screamed and screamed as if my heart were being stabbed with a knife over and over again. I tore at my hair, screaming and crying, but the physical pain kept coming and I couldn't make it stop. My baby brother was dead, shot and killed for protecting one of our cousins from a bully.

Time is fragile. Every second counts. Had my family and I arrived in New Orleans just hours before, I might have had a chance to see my brother still alive. Now he was gone, and nothing could bring him back.

What I didn't know was that my brother's murder was only the first. Within the span of twenty years, all four of my brothers would be dead—victims in unrelated cases of gun violence.

# Chapter Two

## *Life in New Orleans*

Growing up in the projects of the Deep South, I was the overprotective big sister to four boys and one girl. Kimbro, the oldest boy, and I both carried our mother's maiden name, Washington, because our respective biological fathers left while Kimbro and I were still very young. We never had a relationship with either one of them, which was a touchy subject for both Kimbro and me.

Compared with other children in the neighborhood, my family was sheltered. My mother, Althea, made sure of that. For the most part, she kept us inside, because she didn't want us to get into fights or any other sort of trouble. We thought she was overprotective of us, and we didn't have many friends. Althea maintained good discipline in the house.

After my mother married Leonard Phillips, he became our father in every sense of the word. He provided for us, and he was always there for us. Leonard and my mother had four more children together—Leonard Jr., also called "Scooter"; Leniel, nicknamed "Shorty"; my sister Yvonne, and Lamont.

Kimbro loved to eat. My aunt's macaroni was a favorite dish of his, and he liked drinking cold, giant colas. He was popular and a natural people person; he had a lot of friends at school. So did my third brother Leniel, whom everyone called "Shorty" because he was indeed short. Leniel was a charmer, a classic "Momma's boy," and well-loved by everyone. He used to gather up money and fill his pockets with whatever small gifts he could find from around the house and bring them to his teachers at the childcare center, which only made them love him more. They thought he was a little baby doll, with his great big eyes and curly hair.

Leonard was quiet, though he loved to dance. His favorite song was "Kung Fu Fighting." While we all were decent students, Leonard did especially well in school, and Lamont—the youngest—was smarter than all of us. A regular chatterbox, Lamont had a knack for figuring things out, and he was good at math.

"I know how old I'll be when you're twenty-nine," he would say to me. "I'll be sixteen."

Despite my mother's protectiveness, or perhaps because of it, I had my first child at age seventeen. Yvonne, my sister, had her first baby when she was sixteen. My first relationship was very abusive. Once, after my boyfriend beat me, Leonard saw my black eye and grew angry.

"When I grow up, I am going to become a police," he said to me, "and I'm going to put that man in jail."

That sweet sentiment warmed my heart. It made me feel tremendously better, knowing that my little brother wanted to protect me.

In 1983, I was nineteen, a single mother of two. My apartment had been burned down by my abusive boyfriend.

The fire destroyed everything I owned. I had nothing. My mother gave a dinner party, and my uncle brought a friend of his named Malcolm, who was a military veteran. I had seen Malcolm once before, when I was seventeen and pregnant with my first child, and I had thought to myself: He is a beautiful man—a knight in shining armor.

I was right. At the dinner party, it was love at first sight between us. Malcolm took my two kids and me shopping and bought us clothes, taking care of us financially after the devastating loss of my apartment. This wonderful man would soon become my husband. We are very much in love with each other. I would rather be homeless with him than rich without him.

Malcolm and I moved to Tacoma, Washington, to give our children a better life. But we visited our family in New Orleans at least once a year, usually around Christmas.

When Lamont started kindergarten, I brought him school clothes from Tacoma. Lamont was so happy, and so was I—just to see that huge smile on his sweet face.

When my father passed away in 1989, it shook up the family. We were devastated by his loss. Leonard Phillips Sr. left a huge hole in our hearts with his departure. And that's when everything began to fall apart.

My mother, Althea, was left alone to work and provide for the family. She briefly moved to Tacoma, Washington—also to give her children a chance at a better life than we had in New Orleans. But since her seven sisters live in Louisiana, homesickness eventually drove her back. The two youngest boys, Leniel and Lamont, were aged fourteen and twelve, respectively, when our father died. In their late teens, they both got into trouble.

Just three years later, we were still reeling from our father's death when tragedy struck again.

# Chapter Three

# *Bullets from a Bully*

*Kimbro Washington*
*DOB: January 29, 1970   DOD: July 13, 1992*

It was a humid July evening when my brother Kimbro stepped off the bus after a long day of working at McDonald's. A people person and a lover of the fast food industry, he was in training to become a manager of the local McDonald's branch. He was a handsome, well-built young man who played football through middle school. Although his dreams of becoming a professional football player were never realized, Kimbro loved life, and he had three sons—the youngest of whom was just two months old.

Our family is especially tight-knit, and we visit each other frequently. On that particular night, instead of going straight home, Kimbro went to his aunt's house in the 8th Ward. There he was told that his little cousin was being bullied by another black man. Ready to protect his cousin, Kimbro—who was of average height but quite muscular and athletic—went out into the darkness. He approached the man and asked him what the problem was.

The two began to fight. The other man bolted and ran into a bar. Rumor has it that the bartender knew the assailant, and he reportedly gave the man a gun. Now armed, the bully exited the bar, pursued Kimbro, and fired two shots. Both bullets struck Kimbro. Upon seeing Kimbro get shot, his terrified young cousin panicked and ran home, too scared to tell anyone what had happened.

Wounded and bleeding, Kimbro flagged down a passing motorist on Eads Street—just around the corner from his mother's house—and climbed into the passenger seat. The driver, a thirty-year-old New Orleans man who has opted to remain anonymous, got as far as the 2300 block of Franklin Avenue. But it was too late. Moments later, Kimbro died in the stranger's car.

To this day, nobody knows the identity of the unknown black man who killed my brother. There were no arrests made, and the exact details of the murder are still sketchy. The murder happened around eleven p.m., so it was pitch black. Nobody could see anything or anyone. Witnesses heard two gunshots—that's all. Too many unanswered questions still haunt my family.

By the time my husband, my kids, and I arrived in New Orleans, Kimbro had been dead for two hours. I felt like the devil had played a trick on me, robbing me of my brother just a short time before I might have had the chance to see him again. My mother was disconsolate. During the funeral procession, one of my grieving cousins jumped into the hearse with Kimbro, and my aunt had to pull him out.

"That's Kimbro's ride, not yours," she told him firmly.

At the funeral, I could not even attend Kimbro's wake. I couldn't. During the funeral service, my legs were shaking so badly that someone had to hold me up. Torn apart with grief, I was so out of it that when I approached his casket, I was taken aback. I did not recognize my brother. For one wild moment, I thought that the body belonged to someone else rather than my beloved Brody.

But it was really Kimbro, and he was dead at just twenty-two years old. Heartbroken and dazed, I was unaware—until my mother told me later—that Leonard became unruly and refused to allow the casket to close on Kimbro until the police were called.

We buried Kimbro in Resthaven Memorial Park cemetery. He left behind his three sons and their mother, his girlfriend, to whom he had been engaged.

We never held another wake for a death in the family, because Kimbro's funeral lasted for two days and we could not bear the extended duration of it. Unfortunately, our family would soon frequent the funeral home too often. Every year following Kimbro's death, I lost another close family member.

In November of 1993, my cousin—the one who had jumped into the hearse with Kimbro's body—was shot and killed. Then, in April of 1994, the cousin whom Kimbro had died to defend was also gunned down.

Although the anguish of my cousins' deaths was intense, I could not have imagined anything more agonizing than losing one of my precious brothers. My heart was broken so deeply that, even decades later, the pain never goes away.

But in September of 1995, it happened again.

# Chapter Four

# *187*

*Leonard Phillips Jr.*
*DOB: December 14, 1972   DOD: September 27, 1995*

Leonard Jr. must have known his killer. That's what investigators said, though nobody ever found out who killed my second brother.

Leonard Jr.—who was called "Scooter" by his friends and family—had lofty dreams. He never forgot that he wanted to become "a police" and protect people, as he had told me when he was younger. He loved nice cars and high-fashion clothes. His appearance was important to him; he was always well-dressed and smelled nice. Eventually he hoped to become a men's clothing designer. Like our father, Leonard was a self-employed Sheetrock hanger, and he liked to drink a cold Heineken beer each evening when he got off work.

Leonard was known as a fun-loving young man with a great sense of humor, and he loved our family parties. He wasn't the sort to acquire enemies. The epitome of a kindhearted gentleman, he truly would have given anyone the shirt off his back. His friends and family loved him, and one of his cousins—the one who had jumped into Kimbro's hearse—was like his twin brother. The two of them used to visit Kimbro's gravesite and sit there for hours to keep him company, just so Kimbro wouldn't be lonely. But in November of 1993, that cousin was shot and killed.

Like many of us, Leonard took these three deaths hard. He didn't know how to deal with that much pain. Leonard was just sixteen when our father died, and then Kimbro was murdered when Leonard was nineteen. Leonard became a father himself at a young age, and by the time he turned twenty-two, he had three sons whom he loved very much. In 1995, he lived across the river on the West Bank of New Orleans with a young lady and her daughter.

My wedding to Malcolm was coming up in December of 1995, and Leonard was supposed to give me away. On September 27th, we had a phone conversation that took a strange turn.

"Don't buy your son no school clothes," Leonard said to me. "I'm going to have a lot of things to give him."

It was an odd comment, but I didn't think anything of it. Unbeknownst to me, Leonard also told his lady friend that, if he was killed, she should give all his clothes to his nephew— my son.

Nobody knows why Leonard was out late on that same September evening, sitting in his idling car by the side of the road on Alvar Street near North Derbigny. It was hot, even after ten p.m., and Leonard had rolled his windows down. Neighbors saw him speaking with an unknown bicyclist. And then they heard gunshots.

Leonard's car rolled forward and crashed into a nearby porch. By the time police arrived on the scene, Leonard was already dead, shot to death by a mysterious assailant.

My husband and I had just gone to bed when the phone rang. I answered it, and the person on the other end of the line informed me that my second baby brother was dead.

I screamed. Malcolm reached across me and seized the phone.

"Who is this?" he demanded.

Our four young children ran into the room. Grabbing at me and crying, they asked me why someone had killed their Uncle Scooter. I didn't have any answers for them. When my mother heard the terrible news, she passed out on the floor.

The police officer who came to my house found out that I was the sister of the deceased. He asked me if Kimbro Washington was my brother as well. Through a disoriented haze of grief, I stared at him.

"Why? Did you find my brother's killer?"

He hadn't. They had no leads, and he was sorry.

I desperately wanted to see Leonard, but Malcolm wouldn't let me go to the crime scene. But my youngest brother Lamont— who was eighteen at the time—ran to the crash site on Alvar Street before the coroner could remove Leonard's body, and what he saw scared him clear through.

"I didn't see Scooter in the car," he said to me when he returned to the house. "I saw myself."

I tried to comfort him, but I added a warning. "God wanted
you to know that could happen to you," I told him.

It had been difficult for me to look at Kimbro's body until
the last moment, at the funeral. But after Leonard's murder, I
asked to see him before the funeral home did anything to his
body.

What I saw shocked me. His face was burned black as tar.
According to the funeral director, the bullets had been fired
from an AK-47 at such close range that Leonard's face actually
caught fire. Although immediate suspicion was placed on the
unidentified bicyclist whom Leonard had been seen speaking
with shortly before his death, the bullets were fired from the
right—from the passenger seat of Leonard's car—as opposed
to the left, the driver's side, where the bicyclist had been.
Someone must have been sitting in the car with Leonard that
night, and that person must have killed him.

The police gave me Leonard's possessions from the night
of his murder. There were a few blood-soaked dollar bills in
his pocket, along with a pager that simply flashed a number:
187.

The number 187 is commonly used among law enforcement
as a code for murder. Gangs use it too—with the same meaning.
Was the number on Leonard's pager meant as a strong warning
from a friend who knew something, or was it a final message
from his killer? Perhaps a sort of sinister calling card?

We may never know. The police had few leads and the trail
went cold all too quickly.

Scooter was laid to rest in the same grave where they had
placed Kimbro. The workers at the graveyard said Kimbro's

body had mummified, perhaps from too much embalmment fluid. They had to break up Kimbro's body in order to lay Leonard next to him. Since one grave digger had known Kimbro, it shook him to see Kimbro in such a lifelike state three years after his death, and it was difficult for the man to go through with the task of breaking up Kimbro's body.

Now Kimbro is no longer alone in the Resthaven Memorial Park cemetery, because his brother Leonard is forever with him. Like Kimbro, Leonard was only twenty-two years old. Both Kimbro and Leonard left behind three sons. Following Leonard's wishes, his lady friend gave my oldest son all of Leonard's clothes—just as Leonard said he would in his final phone conversation with me.

Losing another brother devastated me. I felt weak, sapped of all my strength, as if I could not go on. My youngest son was turning five just three days after Leonard's death, and I couldn't even bring myself to celebrate his birthday. One of my aunts brought him a cake.

"Erica, I know you're hurting," she scolded me firmly, "but you can't forget about your son's birthday."

On December 2nd, my wedding went forward as planned. I married my Malcolm. Because Leonard was not there to give me away, and because Leniel was out of town at the time, Lamont took his place.

After experiencing five deaths too close to home in just six years—three of those deaths within my immediate family— we were all grief-stricken and nervous. A full decade passed without the dark shadow passing over our household, and we dared to breathe. Maybe the storm was over.

So we thought until shortly after celebrating the new year in 2005.

# Chapter Five

# *Deadly Jealousy*

*Leniel J. Phillips*
*DOB: November 3, 1975   DOD: January 12, 2005*

Leniel, the charming momma's boy, was so tiny that, as a toddler, he could walk through the store while holding onto the bottom rack of the grocery basket. He was never short of friends at school. He loved to make people laugh, and he was particularly good at it. Everyone thought he was cute—because of his great big eyes and curly hair and because of his outgoing personality. From a young age, he was good with his hands and could fix almost anything—cars, electronics such as radios and computers, and anything around my mother's house.

Leniel and Lamont, the youngest boys in our family, were best friends. They shared a room together while they were growing up. Like his older brother Leonard, Leniel enjoyed dressing nicely. He also had a great appreciation for men's fashion—particularly shoes. He wanted to become the owner of a shoe store someday.

Leniel was only fourteen when our father died. While our mother worked hard to support our family by herself, Leniel hung out with the wrong crowd and got hooked on drugs. He did some jail time before he made the decision to turn his life around, and he got a job as a Sheetrock hanger.

While he was in prison, Leniel met a woman named Crystal through a fellow inmate. She already had two children, each with different fathers. Leniel also had a daughter from a previous relationship. Leniel and Crystal quickly fell in love, and after Leniel was released on parole, the two were married on August 1, 2003. They moved to the nearby city of Lafayette, which was Crystal's hometown, and lived in a mobile home there.

Their life together was far from idyllic. I did not find out about the wedding until after the fact, when my mother told me over the phone. Personally, I could not stand Crystal, and I never had any kind of a relationship with her. She was a disrespectful woman with a nasty temper. Once, when Leniel took a trip to New Orleans to visit our mother, she grew angry with Leniel and said that she hoped he would be killed. If he was killed, she said, she would burn his body and throw his ashes into the Mississippi River.

One of Crystal's ex-boyfriends, Calvin Stokes—the father of one of Crystal's two children—was violently jealous of Leniel. He repeatedly broke into the couple's mobile home and stole Leniel's clothes. Even though Calvin was significantly taller and bulkier than my brother Shorty (who stood five feet tall and weighed only 100 pounds), Leniel liked to wear big clothes, and so Calvin took them for his own use.

On January 12, 2005, I received a phone call from Leniel. He needed a bag from my oldest son, who—at the time—was living in another apartment in the same complex with me in Houston, Texas. Leniel left a message for my son, stating that it was important to get back to him. Since my son's phone was broken, I sent my youngest son to verbally deliver Leniel's message.

"I'm going to call my mother," I told my husband, Malcolm, in a phone conversation. He was working out of town. "I haven't spoken with her today."

After he hung up, I made the call. Much to my surprise, my cousin Jerry picked up.

"What are you doing at my mother's house?" I asked.

"You don't want to know," he answered gravely.

I was alarmed. "What's going on?"

"Shorty got shot."

Crystal's ex-boyfriend, Calvin Stokes, had gotten into a heated argument with Leniel. Stokes left the mobile home, then came back a short time later with a loaded .22. He shot at Leniel, who took off running. All six bullets struck my brother from the back, and the bullet that tore through both of his lungs—and then his heart—killed him.

Another death scream tore out of me. My youngest son ran to the neighboring apartment and brought his brother, my oldest son, who frantically dialed Leniel's cell phone number. It was too late. The call would never be returned.

I called Malcolm and begged him to come home, and then I cried all night long. I took two Tylenol PM tablets, but I still could not sleep. The next day, exhausted with grief, I fell asleep in the airport while waiting to board a flight to New Orleans. Someone had to shake me awake before the plane left without me. When I finally arrived at my mother's house, I went inside and fell to the floor, wrapping my arms around her legs and sobbing.

"Erica," my mother said to me in a gravelly tone, "we have walked this road before. God knew all about this day."

Like his two brothers who had been murdered before him, Leniel was also buried at Resthaven Memorial Park cemetery. He was just twenty-nine years old, and he left behind his widow Crystal, her two children, and his daughter. Sadly, the last time my two youngest brothers—Leniel and Lamont—saw each other, they were riding a prison bus together. The next time Lamont saw his older brother was at Leniel's funeral. Lamont's face was blank, his dark eyes staring. His best friend was dead.

For the next two weeks, I could barely eat anything. After I returned to Houston, I couldn't sleep without the aid of Tylenol PM. The loss of three brothers was too much for me, and I felt like I was dying inside. I lost twenty-five pounds and my bowels locked up. The only thing that kept me going was the thought that I could not leave my bereaved mother, my husband Malcolm, or my children; they still needed me. For weeks, Malcolm beseeched God for help on behalf of his wife and his family. All of my brothers had treated Malcolm as if he were a fifth brother—that's how close we were. Leniel's tragic loss was hard on Malcolm on a personal level.

Calvin Stokes was caught and tried for manslaughter. Since he was so much bigger than Leniel, there was no reason for Stokes to have gone after my short little brother with a gun. It was a senseless murder, and yet—as I sat through the trial—I wrestled with conflicting emotions. I found myself feeling sorry for the young man who had killed my baby brother. Then I was angry with myself. How could I feel sorry for the person who had stolen my brother's life and brought our family so much pain? It must have been a grace from God that I felt compassion for Leniel's killer, and yet I felt as if that same sense of compassion somehow dishonored Leniel. Was my sympathy for my brother's murderer a kind of betrayal to him, to his memory?

Calvin Stokes was convicted of manslaughter, and he was sentenced to thirty-five years in prison. To this day, I wish fervently that Leniel had never met Crystal. If he hadn't, perhaps my little brother would still be alive.

# Chapter Six
## *Attempted Robbery*

*Lamont L Phillips*
*Dob: February 17,1977   Date of Death: January 4,2012*

It was December of 2011, and the whole family was tense. One of our cousins, Brandon Butler, had been killed by his girlfriend during a domestic dispute. The all-too-familiar shadow of death that fell over our family brought with it a strange sense of foreboding, which seemed to latch onto my youngest brother, Lamont.

There had always been an odd morbidity that followed Lamont—perhaps because he was only twelve when our father passed away. When Lamont was fifteen, during an intense winter storm in New Orleans, my car broke down just half a mile away from our house. My husband, one of my little sons, and my two youngest brothers—Leniel and Lamont—were forced to leave our vehicle alongside Interstate I-10 and walk home in the freezing cold.

Gusts of icy wind were so strong that they threatened to knock us over, biting at our faces and chilling us all to the bone. We were frozen. The trip seemed to take hours, and we were all miserable—but none more so than Lamont.

"Leave me," Lamont said to me. "Just let me die. I can't make it."

Leniel laughed outright at Lamont, but I tried to reason with my youngest brother. "Do you want Momma to kill me? I will never leave you." Motioning to Leniel and my own son, I added, "Look at Shorty and Noonie. They're not giving up. Man up."

When Lamont was eighteen, our brother Leonard was murdered. Lamont was the one who had seen his dead brother in the crashed car, and he had told me that he had seen himself in Leonard's place. The warning I had given him—that God wanted Lamont to know that the same thing could happen to him—was not without merit.

Then Leniel, Lamont's brother and best friend, was shot and killed shortly before Lamont's twenty-eighth birthday. The painful loss hit Lamont hard.

"I don't have any brothers left," he said to me. The agony I felt increased because I, his big sister, was helpless to ease his pain. Even if I had not been dealing with my own grief, there was nothing I could do to bring our boys back to life.

In spite of the shadow that followed Lamont's life, he was a gentle giant who usually kept his feelings to himself. Family members called him "Rooster Red" on account of his reddish skin tones, but my pet names for him were "Monchie" and "Lamunchie." A habitually rapid talker, most people—

including myself—occasionally couldn't understand him. We had to ask Lamont to slow down and take his time with expressing himself.

Lamont had several different jobs. As a teenager, he worked for a time at Subway. Although he enjoyed it, Lamont was the sort of man who wanted a good life. He was smart and talented enough to succeed at greater opportunities, and he knew it.

Women considered him a "hot piece"; they loved his bald head and sexy lips, and they called him "King Mont." Lamont was aware that he was good-looking eye candy. He loved women as much as they loved him and, in 2008, he got married. Lamont and his wife each had a son from a previous relationship, and then they had a third son together—Lamont Jr. But when Lamont's wife's cousin murdered one of our cousins in October of the same year, the couple divorced a short time later. Lamont never remarried.

Like Leniel, bright young Lamont had also gotten into drugs in the wake of our father's death. He became a heroin addict. In 2000, just five years after Leonard's death, Lamont was convicted of dealing cocaine and was sentenced to fifteen years in prison.

Because of his incarceration, Lamont quit heroin cold turkey. He began working as a plumber and studied hard at school to acquire his license. A handful of cousins and friends, along with Lamont, got together and formed a band called 8/9 Boyz. One of their songs, "More Than Friends," reached the Billboard Top 100 and enjoyed heavy radio airplay, and they were just beginning to taste success. The skies of possibility opened up for Lamont until that cold December in 2011, when the news of our cousin Brandon's murder hit us hard.

Brandon had been a particularly good friend of Lamont. Two more of Lamont's friends had also been killed in previous months.

On New Year's Day 2012, Lamont came to visit my family and me at our home in New Orleans. My grandchildren and both of my daughters were there. I had cooked New Year's dinner, and I was playing a card game—crazy eights—with my husband and one of our daughters. Lamont entered the room and sat next to me.

"I love you," he said to me, and he smiled.

I responded in kind, and Lamont got up and went into the back bedroom to watch television with my other daughter. They spoke quietly for a short time. Then Lamont returned, sat next to me again, and watched us play our card game.

Finally Lamont rose. "I am leaving now," he announced. "I love y'all."

A warm chorus of "I love you too" echoed throughout the house. Lamont made his way to the door, then hesitated. Turning back, he looked at each one of us with a strange intensity.

"What's up, brother-in-law?" asked Malcolm. "Is something wrong?"

Lamont shrugged that off. "No, I'm good," he answered, and then he left.

I returned to my apartment in Houston, Texas, on January 2nd. The next day, on January 3rd, I got a text message from Lamont.

"Tell [your daughter] happy BIRTHDAY because I don't have her number," he sent. I relayed the message to my daughter, but she had no chance to thank her uncle, because I would never hear from Lamont again.

Two days after his visit with my family and me, Lamont met with another cousin named Zulu at a place called Golden Feather—a Mardi Gras Indian gallery that Zulu owned and operated with the help of his wife. Zulu, also a member of Lamont's 8/9 Boyz group, was a Yellow Pocahontas chief who traveled the world as an Indian and a stilt dancer. Between the burgeoning success of 8/9 Boyz and the recent murders of Lamont's two friends and his cousin, Lamont felt like a change was in order.

"I need to get out of that environment," he confided to Zulu.

So Zulu shared an idea with Lamont—the possibility of bringing the 8/9 Boyz on his family's next African tour. Lamont was thrilled. Immediately he agreed, and he left Golden Feather happy.

Later that same night, my daughter-in-law—who was picking up her son, my grandson, from my Houston apartment—got a phone call from her mother.

"Girl, they got some people out here fighting," she said to my daughter-in-law. "I hear gunshots."

None of us knew that one of the people involved in that fight was Lamont. That night, Lamont ran into some recent acquaintances of his. The circumstances of that encounter remain a mystery, but there was a scuffle, then gunshots. When it was all over, my brother Lamont was critically wounded.

It was my niece who called me and told me that Lamont had been shot. "But he's okay," she added in the same breath, smothering the scream that threatened to burst out of me.

Lamont wasn't okay. At ten p.m., paramedics found Lamont on North Tonti Street—about three blocks from his mother's house—and rushed him to University Hospital. Two hours later, Lamont was dead.

My mother called me. "Your baby brother is gone," she said brokenly. "I don't have any more sons left."

We were told that robbery may have been a motive in my brother's shooting. Drugs were found at the scene. After a brief investigation, police arrested two brothers named Don and Antoine Brooks on charges of murder. A detective told me that the Brooks brothers were known drug dealers and thieves who had been on a killing spree since November of 2011, and that the police had been building a case on the two boys. The arrests came too late to save my baby brother from the same fate.

Anger roared through me. "I just wish you had gotten them rotten-ass murderers off the street," I told the detective. "Then my mother's baby would still be alive."

To this day, I do not know why Lamont socialized with the Brooks brothers. According to reports, Lamont had met the brothers just one month earlier. But Lamont was on parole and he had gotten a job that paid well. He had good things happening for him. We have no reason to believe that Lamont was involved with the Brooks brothers' drug dealings.

During the subsequent trial, Don and Antoine Brooks were laughing. Neither showed any remorse for what they had done to their victims or the pain they had caused to several families, including my own.

Both brothers were found guilty. Don was sentenced to sixty years in prison, while Antoine was given twenty-five years.

My last precious brother was buried in Resthaven, along with Kimbro, Leonard Jr., and Leniel. Only the women of my family were left—my mother, Althea, and my younger sister, Yvonne. Lamont left behind two sons and a stepson.

Perhaps Lamont had known that the end was near. Reflecting back on his final visit with us, just two days before he was killed, it seemed like Lamont had paused in the doorway to look at us all for the last time—as if he were silently telling us good-bye.

# Chapter Seven

# *Resthaven*

Dark wishes haunted me—that the Lord would have taken me instead of my brothers, so that my mother could have had at least one of her sons left alive; or that I too would die so that I could be reunited with my brothers. It is the living whom I now live for. My husband needs me. My children need me. And now I have grandchildren.

The murders that stole my brothers from me have been devastating to this day. The grief and anguish are a continual, inescapable torture. As recently as February of 2016, my husband Malcolm and I visited the McDonald's where Kimbro used to work, and I broke down and cried. All my husband could do was look at me and shake his head. Some wounds never heal.

When someone dies, the strongest focus of comfort and support is directed onto the bereaved mother—as perhaps it should. But in the midst of tragedy, fathers and siblings of a lost loved one fade into the background. Immediate family members all feel the agony and suffer the aftereffects; for example, I developed high blood pressure and asthma in the wake of my brothers' deaths.

Some days are harder than others. I look at other people, trying to see my brothers in them—to catch a glimpse of my brothers among the living, even just for a moment. One of my grandsons takes after Leonard, but he mostly reminds me of Lamont, because he has no filter on what he says.

The remaining members of my family used to be so close, but now we rarely see each other. The pain is still too real. We have all drifted apart, and we deal with our grief alone, in our own ways.

The sons and daughters of Kimbro, Leonard Jr., Leniel, and Lamont have grown up and had children of their own. As a grandmother myself, the knowledge that my brothers will never see their beautiful grandchildren—or feel pride as parents and grandparents as they watch these babies mature into wonderful, unique people—is pure anguish. So much life was stolen away from my brothers by such small things as bullets, driven by such evils as jealousy, greed, hatred, and—worst of all—random, senseless violence.

In mainstream society, such emphasis is being placed on "Black Lives Matter." Indeed they do, but all lives are equally precious in the eyes of our Creator. I fervently wish that people would passionately declare that "All Lives Matter," and that violence among every race would come to an end.

My brothers made their share of mistakes. Who hasn't? But they didn't deserve to die. Leniel and Lamont were both in the process of turning their lives around and climbing out of the dark, desolate pit that is drug addiction when they were killed. Their fate is neither right nor fair.

The bullets that were fired at my brothers struck the hearts of many more people—their mother, their sisters, their aunts and uncles and cousins; friends, lovers, children, and the grandchildren whom they will never see. Great holes were torn in the rich tapestry of our family tree, and they can never be repaired. Justice is not even enough, for although three men now sit in jail for murder, no court sentence can bring my brothers back to life.

All four of my brothers now lie in Resthaven, their graves unmarked. It is my hope to provide proper headstones for them someday. Their memories deserve at least that much. Part of the destruction that Hurricane Katrina wreaked on New Orleans in 2005 were the police and coroner records on three of my brothers, since their murders took place in the days before computer records became commonplace. Only paperwork on Leniel, who was living in Lafayette, still remains.

Life marches on without my brothers, and so does our family—like a man who perseveres after the loss of his limbs. But as with amputated limbs, my brothers can never be replaced, and the missing pieces in our family remain a source of constant grief. My brothers' children grew up without fathers. Their grandchildren never knew them. For those of us who were privileged to know them, those four men will be forever missed, and they will remain forever young in our memories.

# Chapter Eight

# *Hope for the Murder Capital of the World*

In New Orleans, we have a rich history and deep roots. Family and heritage hold tremendous meaning for us. We celebrate life with colorful exuberance. Death is not seen as the end, but as a new beginning.

We have special funeral traditions that are unique to our city and our community. After the wake and the funeral, family and friends of the deceased gather for the repass—a meal commonly shared at the family home or at a church, giving the loved ones time to reconnect with each other and give one another comfort and hope. It is a moment to bond, to look ahead to the future, and to move on into a new chapter of our lives—whatever that chapter may be.

Then we have the second line procession, so-called because the procession is traditionally led by a brass band—the "main line" or the "first line." The people who follow the band are called the "second line." This colorful parade floods the streets of New Orleans with marching friends and family members, all accompanied by music, singing, and dancing. Many participants wear colorful costumes, and some stroll along while twirling parasols or handkerchiefs—a form of dancing referred to as "second-lining." The second line itself is a remembrance, a joyful celebration of our lost one's life, and it marks the passage of a dear one's soul between this life and the next.

Second lines can be held for any special occasion, not just funerals. There are second lines for weddings, for grand openings of new businesses, and for gatherings of local clubs. Most Sundays in New Orleans see second lines wending through the city, appearing with the blast of trumpets and the thumping of drums and taking over whole blocks for several minutes. Longer parades include stops at local bars for beer, barbecue, and other refreshments. Sidewalk vendors sell soft drinks, street food, and souvenirs. Many tourists join second lines to experience the unique flavor of New Orleans culture.

The worst tragedy is that New Orleans sees far more second lines for death than for life. Many of those deaths are murders. Over the span of two decades, my family marched in too many second lines—each time with thinner ranks. But statistically, my four brothers were a tiny drop in a vast ocean. In 1992, the year Kimbro was killed, there were 285 murders in New Orleans. In 1995, Leonard Jr.'s death was one of 365 New Orleans murders that year.

Gun violence is all too common in our streets. Drugs run rampant, ensnaring our children and destroying their lives and leading to more violence. Gangs form, competing for territories to sell drugs. At the time of Lamont's murder, we were aware that rivals from another neighborhood had vowed to kill one man per week from the "T-Block," which is bordered by Almonaster Avenue and North Tonti Street. The T-Block was home to my brothers and me, and Lamont was killed on North Tonti Street.

What opportunities do the young men and women of New Orleans have? The focus of our politicians and city leaders is tourism. Their priority is maintaining Bourbon Street and other local attractions, places where visitors can experience the rare beauty of our colorful traditions. In the process, the people who live in New Orleans—the very people who brought those colorful traditions to New Orleans in the first place—have fallen by the wayside.

In spite of thriving tourism in our city, New Orleans is economically depressed. The failure begins with our education system. We need better schools, and with them, better teachers. As it stands, Louisiana was ranked 47th in the country in 2015 overall (according to student test scores), 44th in school system quality, and 43rd in school safety. This is not a new trend.

Without good job opportunities, there is little motivation for our youth to excel as students. Even if they worked hard to acquire a good education, what would they do with it? Where could they put that education to work? Our politicians need to look at that problem and decide how to bring in big corporations that would hire well-educated young men and women for more than minimum wage.

Kids see pushing drugs as an easy way to get ahead, and in a city where people are desperate for money, the temptation proves too great to resist.

New Orleans families are too often broken by divorce, but our families are also broken just as often by violence. My brothers' lives were prime examples of that, and now my brothers' sons are growing up in broken homes because their fathers were murdered.

Overworked single mothers, who are struggling to provide a decent living for themselves and their children, have little time to supervise their teenagers or hold them accountable. That makes it all too easy for kids in school to experiment with drugs, and then to try their hand at dealing drugs to support an expensive and highly addictive habit. Once they step over the criminal line, where do they stop?

With so many people experiencing the effects of murder and violence at a young age, our kids are angry and hurting. Even if they don't come from broken homes themselves, they know other kids who do. And they all know friends and relatives who have been killed before their time. Struggling through the formative years of puberty is hard enough on its own, but our kids also have to deal with tragedies that nobody should have to see.

In response to the pain, they lash out. Disagreements and fights too often end in bloodshed. Teenagers acquire guns of their own—as often for personal protection as for revenge. Their vengeance may steal the lives of innocents, and thus the cycle of violence spreads and takes root in new territory.

Teenagers with guns are a dangerous combination. They have no restraints and no rules—especially when they have grown up in broken homes, where discipline was meted out by harried mothers who are exhausted from working long hours at low-paying jobs just to keep food on the table. Relationships that end in breakups are often ended more permanently with murder. Bullets are the common response to cheating. Domestic disputes end in stabbings and shootings.

Our children have learned by example that their response to arguments or disrespect of any kind should be violence. After they have grown up, nobody teaches them otherwise.

Right now, in New Orleans, there is no street that has not been touched by darkness. There is no ground that has not been splattered with blood and tears. There is no safe place. Only those who are buried at cemeteries like Resthaven find true peace away from the chaos and the grief.

Is it any wonder that more and more families are leaving New Orleans, like mine did? Who would want to raise their children in a city they call "the murder capital of the world"? What parents would be satisfied with substandard education systems that are overrun with drugs, gangs, and guns? What mother would want to listen to her talented kids dream of becoming fashion designers and world leaders, only to watch them end up working in minimum wage jobs like McDonald's or pushing drugs in the dead of night?

My prayer is that New Orleans will see rebirth. How many more innocents have to die before the senseless violence ends? We have fundamental problems that contribute to crime and delinquency in our streets, but those fundamental problems are solvable. All we need are people, especially people in positions of leadership and power, to step up and work hard to provide those solutions. New Orleans is waiting.

Will you be the one to help us?

My four brothers did not have to die. But if their short lives serve as lessons to prevent other families from losing sons and daughters, then their deaths were not in vain. Their memories will have purpose. My brothers will be four sparks that bring light into dark city streets, and they will be the catalyst to restore hope into hearts that have forgotten hope in the midst of grief.

My prayer is that Kimbro, Leonard Jr., Leniel, and Lamont's deaths will not be the end, but a new beginning—for the whole city of New Orleans.

www.ingramcontent.com/pod-product-compliance
Lightning Source LLC
Chambersburg PA
CBHW060656280326
41933CB00012B/2202